PARANORMAL
INVESTIGATIONS

The Bermuda Triangle, Stonehenge,

and Unexplained Places

Andrew Coddington

Cavendish Square

New York

Published in 2018 by Cavendish Square Publishing, LLC
243 5th Avenue, Suite 136, New York, NY 10016

Website: cavendishsq.com

This publication represents the opinions and views of the author based on his or her personal experience, knowledge, and research. The information in this book serves as a general guide only. The author and publisher have used their best efforts in preparing this book and disclaim liability rising directly or indirectly from the use and application of this book.

Cataloging-in-Publication Data

Names: Coddington, Andrew.
Title: The Bermuda Triangle, Stonehenge, and unexplained places / Andrew Coddington.
Description: New York : Cavendish Square Publishing, 2018. | Series: Paranormal investigations | Includes index.
Identifiers: ISBN 9781502628435 (library bound) | ISBN 9781502628442 (ebook)
Subjects: LCSH: Geographical myths--Juvenile literature. | Stonehenge (England)--Juvenile literature. | Bermuda Triangle--Juvenile literature.
Classification: LCC GR940.K55 2018 | DDC 398.23'4--dc23

Editorial Director: David McNamara
Editor: Kristen Susienka
Copy Editor: Rebecca Rohan
Associate Art Director: Amy Greenan
Designer: Joseph Macri
Production Coordinator: Karol Szymczuk
Photo Research: J8 Media

Printed in the United States of America

Contents

Although science has shed light on many of the world's mysteries, there are several places, such as Stonehenge, that remain unexplained.

A Dive into History

Humans have been exploring the world around them since our ancestors first stepped out of caves and into the open air. At first, many did so in order to find resources to live a better life. Scientists believe that today's species of humans, called *homo sapiens*, which in Latin translates into "wise man," first originated in Africa approximately two hundred thousand years ago. These early humans spread out from their homelands in search of areas with more fertile soil, better hunting, a more comfortable climate, or to get away from rival clans. This migration took humans out of Africa and into the Middle East, and from there to Europe and Asia and, eventually, all the way to the Americas, and even remote islands in the Pacific Ocean. Today, humans live on every continent, including Antarctica, the coldest and most hostile place to humans on Earth.

Movement seems like an innate human need. As the saying goes, the grass is always greener on the other side of the fence, and so people press on, exploring new lands. In today's world, however, it seems like the entire planet has already been explored. People romanticize about the great European Age of Exploration, lasting between the fifteenth and seventeenth centuries. During this time, people wondered what existed

A network of global positioning system (GPS) satellites orbiting Earth has documented every corner of our planet's surface.

outside their narrow scope of the world, imagining lands filled with untold riches and protected by seas haunted by monsters. Sailors and sea captains left their homes to sail into the unknown, uncharted waters that lay beyond the horizon. Today, it would seem their work is complete. Humans instead have turned their attention to space, calling it the "final frontier." Global positioning system (GPS) satellites orbit Earth, charting every possible corner of the world, and scientists working around the world have categorized and explained all of the world's mysteries … Or have they?

Mysteries of the Deep

As much as we have already explored, we still have a narrow scope of the world. For example, living on land, it may seem like we have a pretty clear understanding of the world we find ourselves in. If one looks at a map of their home country, the United States or Canada for example, it may seem like those countries take up a huge amount of Earth's surface. This isn't wrong: the United States and Canada both take up about 3.8 million square miles (9.8 million square kilometers) each. However, the whole world measures approximately 197 million square miles (510 million sq km), and over 70 percent of that is water. This means that nearly 140 million square miles (360 million sq km)—or eighteen times the area of the United States and Canada *combined*—is water.

Water, unlike land, takes up three-dimensional space. Generally speaking, a person on land can only move around on one plane—horizontally—but a creature in the water can travel in two planes—horizontally and vertically. This is because water, unlike land, has depth. Most of the water on Earth is contained in the oceans. The average depth of the ocean is about 12,100 feet (3,688 meters), or 2.3 miles (3.7 kilometers), but there are even greater depths. The deepest part of the ocean is called the Challenger Deep, which is located along the southern end of the Mariana Trench in the Pacific Ocean. Here, depths reach up to a staggering 36,200 feet (11,033.76 m), or 6.8 miles (11 km).

Oceans are obviously big places, so it should be no surprise that we have explored only the barest sliver of them. Even with all of humanity's advanced technologies, such as sonar and manned and unmanned submarines capable of withstanding the crushing pressure experienced at great depths, we have only explored a measly 5 percent of the seas, according to **oceanographers**. This means that humans have little to no idea of 95 percent of the oceans surrounding our continents.

Ancient Mysteries

What is contained in the expanse of the oceans is just one of the world's many great mysteries, and one of the greatest puzzles revolves around something else entirely: ourselves. As much as we don't understand about the seas, there is perhaps even less that we know about the history of humanity itself. As previously mentioned, *homo sapiens* have been on Earth for thousands of years. However, humans have only been able to record their histories through writing for a fraction of that time. Writing was invented first in 3200 BCE in Mesopotamia in modern-day Iraq, and later independently by the Mesoamerican culture known as the Olmecs in 600 BCE. This means that humans have only been able to record their histories through writing for barely more than $\frac{1}{100}$th of the time they have been on Earth.

Archaeologists, such as these digging in Orkney off the coast of Scotland, work to explain the parts of ancient history that have been lost to us.

Not everything about humanity's early history is completely dark, however. Fortunately for people interested in **anthropology**, or the study of human cultures, written history is not the only source for knowledge about ancient peoples. Ancient people, intentionally or not, left clues about their cultures that help shed light on humanity's origins and the paths that our ancestors took to where we are today. These clues assume many forms, including physical artifacts such as pottery, tools, and weapons; human remains, such as bones and mummified or otherwise preserved bodies; and artwork, such as jewelry, cave paintings, and stone arrangements. Whether it seems obvious or not, each of these things tells a story. When anthropologists discover such clues, they approach them like a crime scene investigator might. They ask questions such as: Who left this here? Why? Who made it and when? What purpose did this object serve? In answering these questions, scientists put together a picture, bit by bit, of the object, the person who used it, and the roles both of them played in their societies.

Unexplained Places

Of the world's greatest mysteries, two have proved perpetually puzzling to people throughout the ages. Each of these come from the great unexplored corners of the sea and human history. They are the Bermuda Triangle and Stonehenge.

As little as we know about the ocean in general, there is one thing that's certain: something isn't quite right in the area between Bermuda, Florida, and Puerto Rico. These three points make up what is known as the Bermuda Triangle or, sometimes, the Devil's Triangle. Unexplained occurrences have been happening in this approximately 1.5-million-square-mile (2,414,016 sq km) stretch of the Atlantic Ocean since as early as

1492, when Christopher Columbus was exploring the region in search of a westward passage to India. Since then, the Bermuda Triangle has been the site of an unusually high number of maritime tragedies: dozens of ships and planes have wrecked here, and there are even several cases of disappearances. Somehow, people, crews, and even whole ships and planes have been known to vanish—all without sending out distress signals, all without leaving a trace.

In addition to the Bermuda Triangle, another of the world's most awe-inspiring unexplained locations is Stonehenge. Located in Wiltshire, England, Stonehenge is a prehistoric monument dating back to about 2500 BCE. It consists of a ring of **menhir**, or standing stones, which are placed in earthen mounds. Just because Stonehenge can be found on good old terra firma does not mean it is any less of a mystery than the Bermuda Triangle. Everything from its construction, materials, and purpose seems to defy explanation, and the closer scientists look at the **megalith**, the more questions it seems to pose. How was it that a prehistoric people lacking common tools managed to mine, transport, and erect the stones, each of which weighs about 25 tons (23 metric tons)? How did this ancient culture manage to build a monument that seems to correspond so accurately with the movement of the solar system? Why was it built? And why have **cremated** human remains been found throughout the site?

Humanity has advanced so far, so quickly in its relatively short time on Earth. There is no doubt that our technologies and intellect have earned our species the name "wise man." However, it is all too easy for people to think that impressive technology and intellect have made us masters of the world around us. The reality is that for as much as we know, there remains many times more that we do not know at all. Between the depths of the ocean and the depths of humanity's collective memory, there are still mysteries left in the world. It's time to take a deeper dive.

Despite modern humans' advanced technology, 95 percent of the ocean remains unexplored.

The Bermuda Triangle has been the site of countless shipwrecks, plane crashes, and disappearances.

CHAPTER ONE

The Graveyard of the Atlantic

The Bermuda Triangle has been the stuff of legends and folktales for centuries, but despite some of the more outlandish yarns, the fact remains that the 1.5 million square mile (2,414,016 sq km) wedge of the mid-Atlantic has claimed the lives of thousands of pilots and sailors. In the past one hundred years, more than one thousand souls have been lost in its waters, and on average, five aircraft and twenty-five sailing vessels disappear every year.

A History of Mystery

Stories about the unusual nature of the Bermuda Triangle are as old as the recorded history of the area. Christopher Columbus, who explored the Americas during his famous voyage in 1492, reported witnessing strange happenings during his leg through the waters between Florida, Bermuda, and Puerto Rico. Among these occurrences were unexplained malfunctions of his navigation equipment as well as startling lights that appeared in the sea. (For more, see: "Columbus's Voyage" on page 16.)

Columbus's journey to the Caribbean (which he called the West Indies, and its inhabitants Indians, because he mistakenly believed he had landed in India and not an entirely new continent) sparked intense interest among the rulers of Europe's most powerful nations. All of them wanted to colonize these new lands and exploit their wealth. As a result, sea traffic between Europe and the Americas exploded in the sixteenth and seventeenth centuries. Oceangoing ships transported colonists from Europe and Africa to the New World, and wealth and raw materials from the New World back to Europe. This process was known as the Triangular Trade and made the European nations that colonized the West Indies wealthy—at the expense of Africans and Native Americans.

It is unclear how many other ships experienced unusual events in the Bermuda Triangle as Columbus had, though it seems likely that many did given the increase in traffic in the area immediately following Columbus. It is customary for ships to keep a **log**, which is a daily record of the ship's position, weather and other atmospheric measurements, and notable events onboard. Logs are primarily tools for insurance purposes, since ships and their cargoes are expensive investments that their owners want to protect. However, logs also provide interesting information to historians about the day-to-day life aboard vessels, acting almost like a ship's diary. Unfortunately, many ships' logs, like countless other historical documents, have been lost or destroyed in the decades and centuries since they were written.

Outside of Columbus's log, there is little concrete evidence about the early history of the Bermuda Triangle, but there is one story of note. It concerns a man named Thomas Lynch Jr., who was born in the British colony of South Carolina in 1749. Lynch represented his home state at the Second Continental Congress and even signed his name to the Declaration of Independence in 1776 before falling ill. In 1779, Lynch endeavored to travel to France to seek therapeutic treatment for his sickness. However, having just committed treason, Lynch knew he could not cross the Atlantic in an American ship, so he sailed south to the West Indies, where he expected to board a neutral ship. Unfortunately, Lynch's yacht never reached its destination, and no part of the ship was ever recovered. Lynch's passage from South Carolina to the Caribbean would have taken him directly through the Bermuda Triangle, however, leaving some to wonder.

The Last Voyage of the USS *Cyclops*

One of the most tragic stories attributed to the mystery of the Bermuda Triangle revolves around the USS *Cyclops* in World War I. *Cyclops* was a US Navy collier, a cargo ship designed to transport coal, which was the primary fuel for naval ships at the time. On January 8, 1918, *Cyclops* departed Norfolk, Virginia, for Rio de Janeiro, Brazil, with nearly 10,000 tons (9,071 metric tons) of coal to supply allied British ships operating in South America. On February 15, she departed Rio de Janeiro laden with 11,000 tons (9,979 metric tons) of manganese ore (manganese is used in the manufacture of steel), stopping briefly in Bahia, Brazil, before departing for a nonstop voyage to Baltimore, Maryland. The *Cyclops* was forced to stop at the Caribbean island of Barbados, however, because her captain complained that the starboard (right-side) engine had catastrophically malfunctioned, reducing the ship's speed to 10 knots, potentially as a result of being overladen in Brazil. The navy suggested that the *Cyclops* return to the United States for repairs. The passage from Barbados to the US mainland would have taken the *Cyclops* clear across the Bermuda Triangle, with Barbados lying southeast of the triangle's east side. She departed Barbados on March 4 and was due March 13.

COLUMBUS'S VOYAGE

Christopher Columbus sailed through the Bermuda Triangle on his voyage west across the Atlantic in 1492. By the time his fleet returned to Europe, his log was full of incredible stories about new lands and peoples. Among the most puzzling entries, however, occurred in October 1492, while Columbus's fleet was sailing through the waters between Florida and Bermuda. Columbus noted that his compass, which had faithfully pointed toward the North Star the whole voyage, now pointed several degrees to the left. Although that may seem like a relatively minor difference, such a malfunction could prove disastrous to fifteenth-century navigators sailing through uncharted waters. It's possible that even a minor variation in a ship's heading, or direction, could lead the crew many hundreds of miles off course over several days and possibly leave them hopelessly lost at sea. Fortunately for Columbus, he was able to catch this anomaly and adjust for the mistake.

In addition to the unusual behavior of his navigational instruments, Columbus and his crew witnessed something shocking in the waters of the Bermuda Triangle. On October 11, Columbus and at least one other crew member saw a ball of light that seemed to rise from out of the sea. According to the ship's position, they were too far from land to have been able to see a light from shore.

Modern **skeptics** who have read Columbus's account argue that the light probably came from either a meteor crashing into the sea or possibly the rare but natural **phenomenon** known as ball lightning. Ball lightning is a phenomenon in which static electricity in the atmosphere is discharged, but instead of taking the form of a brief bolt of lightning, it takes the form of an orb that can be up to several inches in diameter. Unlike regular lightning, which dissipates almost instantly, ball lightning can appear for up to several minutes and has been documented to behave erratically. For example, some pilots report having been "chased" by orbs of light; these are likely ball lightning, whose electrical charge is attracted to the bodies of aircraft.

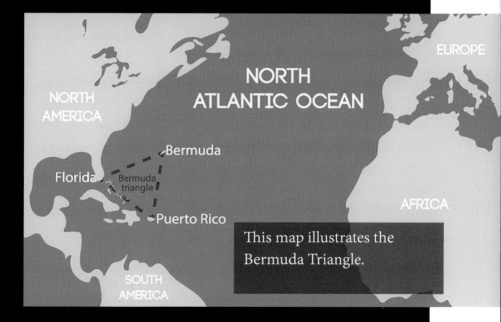

This map illustrates the Bermuda Triangle.

The USS *Cyclops* in 1911, seven years before it disappeared without a trace

The ship never arrived. She and her crew of 309 were lost at sea, disappearing without a trace.

A ship carrying molasses allegedly sighted the *Cyclops* off the coast of Virginia on March 10, three days before she was due to arrive. However, the navy concluded that this was impossible since the ship had approximately 1,800 nautical miles to travel between Barbados and Baltimore, all on a crippled engine. Investigators concluded that the *Cyclops* suffered from a convergence of factors that resulted in its tragic loss. Because the ship's starboard engine was inoperable, it had to rely exclusively on the propulsion of its engine on the opposite side, the port (left) side. Should that engine suffer damage or fail entirely, the *Cyclops* would be stranded at sea. Adding to that, the *Cyclops* had suffered damage to her hull on a previous voyage, which meant that she was likely taking on water. Additionally, her design made her susceptible to rolls on the ocean, a problem that may have been compounded by improperly stored cargo that the *Cyclops* had taken on in

Rio. As a ship travels on the water, it has a tendency to roll, or pitch from one side to the other on its axis. Although this is normal, some ships can roll to extreme degrees, which creates the risk of **capsizing**. This problem can be exacerbated on ships with large cargoes, such as the *Cyclops*, because that weight can become improperly balanced on a journey, increasing the likelihood of more extreme rolls and affecting a ship's buoyancy. Many investigators believe that the ship had slowly been taking on water during its voyage, which went unnoticed by the ship's watch stationed in the bridge high above the hull until it was already too late. Combined with the sudden onset of a second engine failure or a violent **squall** (or both), the *Cyclops* would have been lost in a matter of minutes.

The sinking of the USS *Cyclops* constitutes the greatest loss of life aboard a US-built ship in the history of the US Navy with unknown causes. Although many theories exist, there is no direct evidence to explain what happened and for what reasons. Most puzzling of all, however, is the fact that no piece of the wreck has ever been discovered, and its location remains unknown.

The wreck of the *Cyclops* prompted President Woodrow Wilson to remark, "Only God and the sea know what happened to the great ship."

Flight 19

Losses of sailing vessels are not the only tragedies that have been attributed to the Bermuda Triangle. Many aircraft have been known to disappear without a trace.

One such airborne mystery concerns Flight 19, a squadron of fighter planes that disappeared over the Bermuda Triangle. On December 5, 1945, five Grumman TBM Avenger Torpedo Bombers departed from the US Naval Air Station (NAS) in

GOOD EVENING
It's usually a bundle of nerves that's all wrapped up in worry.

MOUNT CARMEL ITEM

EXCLUSIVE LEASED WIRE DISPATCHES OF THE UNITED PRESS ASSOCIATIONS

WEATHER
Rain ending tonight. Friday fair and warmer.

VOL. LIX. NO. 30.   MOUNT CARMEL, PA., THURSDAY, DECEMBER 6, 1945.   PRICE—FOUR CENTS

BEHIND THE HEADLINES

Germany Keystone On Reconstruction

BY LOUIS F. KEEMLE

Germany remains, even in defeat, a keystone in the problem of reconstructing Europe.

That is why the Big Three—Britain, the United States and Russia—have been in such a row with France over a controlling the Germans to remain some kind of central government of their own. The dispute now seems to be in the process of being laid aside by compromise.

Europe, including Germany, has entered into a winter which promises starvation and untold hardship. The social consequences may set back political and economic recovery on the continent by years if production is not resumed in Germany and neighboring States. Allied commanders have recognized that it must be resumed in Germany since the leading industrial State cannot be removed from the heart of the continent without disastrous consequences both immediate and long-range.

The French have been accused by official Allied sources notably American of blocking progress by their stubborn refusal to consent to a centralized German Government without some measure of dismemberment of western Germany.

The French however have stood by what is to them an unanswerable argument against creating a new German Government which will again control the great industrial areas on either side of the Rhine, with their warmaking potentialities.

The regions concerned are the Ruhr, the Rhineland and the Saar. The French have maintained, and still maintain in the face of strong pressure from the Big Three, that if one areas should be divorced permanently from the Reich and placed under international control.

Otherwise, in the French view, Germany could again become the strongest industrial nation in Europe within a few decades, and could once more attack France under a war-minded government.

The French people cannot forget the three German invasions of their soil by Germany within 70 years, and they are not likely to let any French Government forget it, whether backed by President Charles de Gaulle of someone less nationalistically-minded.

An authoritative French spokesman, assumed but presumably representing the official viewpoint, was quoted in a United Press dispatch:

(Continued on Page Twelve)

Over $1,500 To Be Cleared For Memorial

Net Proceeds Bigger Than Anticipated After Benefit Game

Likely over $1,500, a couple of hundred dollars more than previously expected, will be cleared on the recent Mount Carmel-Mount Carmel Township Living War Memorial Fund post-season benefit football game, it was believed today by officials of the Mount Carmel District Veterans Association trying to give the community a recreational-cultural building in Town Park as a useful and lasting monument in tribute to servicemen and servicewomen of this war.

With certain items like Federal tax on tickets and the cost of a combined dinner or expense dinner for the two high school squads yet to be paid, the net proceeds from the special attraction stand well over $1,600, a detailed financial statement showed this morning.

Receipts totaled $2,124.10 and expenses amounting to $718.45, including the tax to be deducted.

The cost of dinners for the grid teams is expected to run around $100. No date has been set for the affair, or affairs, because Carmen Cavacini, for one, unfortunately was injured in the game. The Mount Carmel quarterback, suffering from a fractured shoulder, has admitted to Ashland State Hospital several days ago.

Officers of the Memorial Association indicated they considered contact a worthwhile effort. If a minimum of helping the descriptive drive for funds, pile a bad weather break resulting in the game being poorly attended. Both weekend up tonight and hangings until the next evening when in cold, instead of raining or slowing, a snowfalls in the final outcome.

The financial report, as related

(Continued on Page Eleven)

FIVE NAVY BOMBERS VANISH

HURLEY CHARGES PLOT TO OUST CHIANG

Shielding his eyes from glare of photographer's lights, Gen. eral Patrick J. Hurley, resigned U. S. ambassador to China, testifies before the Senate Foreign Affairs Committee in Washington too. He shrugged career diplomats in China, led by George Acheson, Jr., wanted to give long-lease arms to Chinese Communists with the deliberate purpose of destroying the Central Government of Generalissimo Chiang Kai-shek.

HURLEY CHARGES POLICY IN IRAN WRECKED BY ACHESON

WASHINGTON, Dec. 6 (UP)—Patrick J. Hurley charged before the Senate Foreign Relations Committee today that Undersecretary of State Dean Acheson had wrecked U. S. foreign policy in Iran.

The resigned ambassador to China widened the scope of his accusations against State Department personnel to include diplomatic activities in Iran.

When he resigned last week, Hurley accused State Department career men of sabotaging U. S. policy in China. It was to divert those charges that he was summoned before the Senate committee. He reiterated the charges yesterday, naming five foreign service officials, and returned to the attack today.

Under questioning by Committee Chairman Tom Connally, D., Tex., Hurley said persons in the State Department had "interfered with and defeated American policy in Iran," where the Iranian government is now trying to put down a revolt.

Hurley once went on a diplomatic mission to Iran for the late President Roosevelt before he became ambassador to China.

Asked by Connally who in the State Department was responsible for wrecking U. S. policy in Iran, Hurley replied that the Indispensable skipper was on the bridge immediately following the explosion.

"What orders did he give?"

"He gave the order to abandon ship. He hollered down from the bridge to the men who were standing on the ship's port side."

As they did yesterday, Hurley and Connally clashed frequently. Hurley insisted he was not attacking the Administration. He said he probably would wind up on the side of President Truman. He volunteered the statement that he had never met Sen. Kenneth S. Wherry, R., Neb., who tried unsuccessfully to block Acheson's appointment as undersecretary.

Hurley told the committee that at the direction of President Roosevelt he prepared "What is known as the Declaration of Three Powers on Iran."

He read the agreement. In it, President Joseph Stalin, Mr. Roosevelt, and former Prime Minister Winston Churchill recognized Iran's contribution in the war effort in meeting

M'Vay Ordered Ship Abandoned

WASHINGTON, Dec. 6 (UP)—Capt. Charles B. McVay, III., ordered his officers and men to abandon the sinking Cruiser Indianapolis, a survivor said today.

McVay is charged by the Navy with failing to issue "timely orders" to abandon the ship before it sank with the loss of 880 of its 1,196 officers and men aboard.

Coxswain Edward H. Keyes of Antigo, Wis., testified at McVay's court martial that he was standing on the bridge following the two explosions which caused the ship to go down within 15 minutes.

Asked if he saw McVay on the bridge, Keyes replied that the Indispensable skipper was on the bridge immediately following the explosions.

"What orders did he give?"

"He gave the order to abandon ship. He hollered down from the bridge to the men who were standing on the ship's port side."

Keyes, who was standing amidships on the bridge, then went below decks to check the ship's loud-speaker and public address system. He said that the explosion had disposed all communications.

He could give no estimate as to how much time elapsed between the time Capt. McVay gave the orders and when the ship went down.

Lt. Comdr. John Reid of New London, N.H., ship's supply officer, said he heard no orders of any kind given at the time of the ship.

Ship's Bugler Donald F. Mack of Easton, Pa., told the court yesterday he was unable to contact the commander's quarters when he telephoned from the bridge where he was located after the explosion.

Gen. Marshall Tells Of Attempt To Build Up Hawaii's Defense

BY JOHN T. CUTTER

WASHINGTON, Dec. 6 (U.P.)—Gen. George C. Marshall said today he robbed training squadrons in the United States of planes with which to build up the air defense of Hawaii early in 1941.

The former Chief of Staff told the Pearl Harbor Investigating Committee of his efforts to build defenses for the Pacific outpost while simultaneously conducting a growing training program at home and supplying Great Britain by her war with Germany.

Marshall was called to tell his story of the Japanese attack Dec. 7, 1941, before he leaves on his new assignment as special diplomatic envoy to China. Spectators in the jammed hearing room greeted him with applause.

Marshall testified that he did not feel at the time that there was any probability of a Japanese attack on the fleet at Pearl Harbor. But, he said, he felt safeguards should be taken against all possibilities.

Records released by the committee disclosed that in June of the previous year, 1940, Marshall had for a time been anxiously fearful of a Japanese attack on Hawaii.

The Army ordered its Hawaiian Commander in June, 1940, to go on war alert "to deal with possible trans-Pacific raid."

The Army's fears, as explained to the Army and Navy commanders in Hawaii, were inspired by the signing of a new Russian-Japanese agreement. The Army felt that the agreement might have been timed to permit the Japanese to attack Pearl Harbor while the U. S. Fleet was absent.

But that attack never materialized and Marshall felt no immediate specific fears in 1941 when he undertook to augment the islands' air defenses.

In reviewing the domestic training program he supplied Hawaii, Marshall disclosed that in February, 1941, he took most of their P-40 pursuit planes away from squadrons in this country.

"I think we cut most of them down to three planes," he said.

Thirty planes were dispatched to Hawaii as a Navy aircraft carrier, without exiting, to save time. The Hawaiian command then had 50.

At the same time, Marshall said, he put pressure on the Curtiss-Wright Corp. at Buffalo, N. Y., for delivery of more new P-40 planes. Forty of them were sent as a carrier from San Diego on March 10,

(Continued on Page Twelve)

Hawaii Alert In 1940 Explained

WASHINGTON, Dec. 6 (UP)—The Army ordered a war alert in Hawaii in June, 1940, because it feared a Japanese raid there, it was disclosed today.

The fear was inspired by the signing of an agreement between Japan and Russia. The agreement was believed to permit the Japanese to attack the U. S. Fleet at Pearl Harbor while it was absent, which John J. G. Richardson, Navy Commander at Pearl Harbor, had testified was never explained to him.

Gen. C. D. Herron, at that time Commander of the Hawaiian Department, received the following War Department orders on June 17, 1940:

"Immediately alert complete defensive organization to deal with possible trans-Pacific raid coming to greatest extent possible without creating public hysteria or provoking

---

BULLETINS

NEW YORK—The Authracite Institute reported today that hard coal production for the calendar year ended Dec. 1 totaled 47,137,887 tons. Output for last week was estimated at 1,112,109 net tons.

GETTYSBURG, Pa. — Betty Wachter, 47, was struck and killed by an automobile today as she left her home to board a bus for Harrisburg, where she is employed by the State Revenue Department.

BATAVIA — British troops rescued several hundred trapped Dutch civilians from the centre of Bandoeng today, after calling up RAF warplanes to blast the Indonesian besiegers from their path. Four British Mosquito bombers swooped now over the Nationalist strongpoint behind the Mountain Hotel and scattered the Indonesians with rockets and gunfire.

WASHINGTON — Congress was told today that this country should adopt compulsory peacetime military training only as a last resort, Edward T. McCaffrey, National Commander of the Catholic War Veterans, told the House Military Affairs Committee that the United States first should attempt to abolish conscription as a whole.

CAIRO — An attempt to assassinate former Egyptian Premier Nahas Pasha was thwarted today.

Two Kulpmont Residents Held Without Bail

Committed To County Jail To Await Trial

Edward Glodek, 32, of 1157 Poplar street, Kulpmont, charged by State Police with arson, was committed by Justice of the Peace H. O. Baranoski, Shamokin, to the county jail to await trial without bail.

Joseph Ondyswind, 17, of 706 Pine street, Kulpmont, charged by State Police as an accomplice of Glodek's in a number of burglaries, also was committed to the county jail to await trial without bail.

State Police said that Glodek, whose first name was erroneously listed as Frank in yesterday's Item, has admitted setting fire to the Evert Lumber Yard, Kulpmont, on the night of May 21, 1940, causing damages estimated $20,000.

Frank Glodek is in the armed forces and a relative and is subdued to return home from Georgia.

At the hearing last night, Glodek and Ondyswind also admitted, State Police said, to the theft of the automobile of Dr. A. J. Ancerawicz, Kulpmont, and the car owned by Philip Brenner, Shamokin. Police also said they also admitted burglarizing the James Madison Hotel, Shamokin, of $80.

The arraignment of Glodek and Ondyswind on the Kulpmont robberies was held before Squire James Avellino. The charges were made by the Kulpmont police.

Veterans Will Meet At Atlas

A meeting of the Atlas ex-servicemen will be held on Sunday afternoon at 2:00 o'clock at the Atlas Hose House.

Rocco Marshall, temporary chairman of the proposed new Legion of Veterans organization, urges all ex-servicemen of the community to attend the meeting. Servicemen home on leave, or furlough, also are invited.

Dr. And Mrs. Wetzel Welcome Son

A baby boy was born to Dr. and Mrs. Leon A. Wetzel of 158 south Market street, Dr. Wetzel is the well known Chiropodist. Mrs. Wetzel was formerly Miss Elizabeth Krmer, of Mervay.

The couple now have two children, both boys.

Speed Up Trial At Nuernberg

BY FREDERICK OECHSNER

NUERNBERG, Dec. 6 (UP)—An admission by Hermann Goering that Germany was actively preparing for war against Poland in August, 1939, while diplomatic efforts to stave off the conflict purportedly were underway was read into the record of the War Crimes tribunal today.

Goering's admission was made during interrogation by American authorities after his capture. Goering's attorneys protested introduction of the interrogation transcript but the court overruled their plea.

Hitler's orders for a surprise invasion of Poland, evidence revealed, were issued five months in advance and actually named the invasion date, Sept. 1, 1939.

British and American prosecution staffs were making every effort to speed presentation of the case. They hoped to complete presentation of evidence under the first two counts

(Continued on Page Eleven)

Two Spanish Spies Sentenced To Jail

PHILADELPHIA, Dec. 6 (UP)—Emilio Sep Cassas Hernandez, 26-year-old Spanish seaman, was under sentence of ten years in Federal prison today after he pleaded guilty to espionage against the United States on behalf of Germany.

Pablo Lagarzia 33, Bilboa, Spain, another seaman was sentenced to one year and one day in prison after pleading guilty to two minor espionage charges.

Judge Harry E. Kalodner imposed the sentences yesterday after a Federal grand jury on an espionage indictment, handed down yesterday, charged them with furnishing information on the movements of Allied warships, and sought information on the Federal Bureau of Investigation for failure to apply the Germans with information on America's war activities.

Searching Plane With 12 Aboard Dives In Flames

BY RICHARD C. GLASS

MIAMI, Fla., Dec. 6 (U.P.) — A Navy Patrol Bomber carrying perhaps 12 men crashed in flames into the Atlantic last night while searching for five Torpedo Bombers which disappeared mysteriously, it was revealed today.

The patrol craft, a "Mariner" from the Banana River Nav I Air Station, crashed off Ponce de Leon Inlet, near Daytona Beach. The Coast Guard here said that flames flared 100 feet into the air and were seen by a merchant vessel.

No wreckage was found in the morning, in a first search of the area, the Coast Guard said. Rescue operations were underway there and a vast search covered all of Florida and nearby waters for the plane. An aircraft carrier joined in the search.

The Torpedo Bombers flew from the Naval Air Station at Fort Lauderdale, Fla., yesterday afternoon and vanished without trace. Today a widespread hunt over thousands of square miles of land and sea was on to restore.

The search for them perhaps was the largest ever organized from the continental United States. Scores of military planes and vessels among them the Escort Aircraft Carrier Solomons, were called out for aid in piercing the mystery and if possible rescuing the men.

The missing planes had not been heard from late yesterday, while no routine flight over the Atlantic Sundewen came and they should have returned, but there was no sign. No radio messages came through and the planes which might have happened.

In Jacksonville, Rear Adm. Ralph E. Davison, Chief of Naval Aviation Operations in the area, ordered an immediate investigation.

His office reported that a ship, the Gaines Mills, reported having seen an explosion some time yesterday but the exact location was not given.

Each of the Torpedo Bombers carried two men, and as many as a dozen may have been aboard the patrol plane.

The weather in the search area generally was fair today, with brisk winds and occasional showers. It was about the same when the planes left.

The planes were believed to have been over the sea on a routine flight, but today the search was also underway at some of the towns of Florida Peninsula. Planes and surface craft patrolled all waters 100 miles to sea, from north of Jacksonville to the Bahamas.

The Escort Carrier Solomons, off the Southeast Florida Coast by daybreak today, lowered its own aircraft and launched her planes this morning.

(Continued on Page Eleven)

General Motors' Parley Resumed

BY ALLEN V. BOWLING

DETROIT, Dec. 6 (UP)—General Motors Corp. and the striking CIO United Auto Workers Union sought today to chart a path to labor peace. They were working against time in an effort to solve their differences before the federal government takes a hand in the 18-day-old walkout of 175,000 GM employes.

The explosive 30 per cent wage increase demand by the UAW which precipitated the strike Nov. 21 was laid on the Union-Corporation conference table for renewed discussion for the first time since the walkout stoppage began. Collective bargaining conferences between the two opposing sides had been re-established yesterday at the UAW resume at 2 p.m. today.

Agreement to resume full collective bargaining "with no strings attached" was reached yesterday at a dramatic, strongly-worded conference on Union-Corporation differences. In Pittsburgh earlier CIO President Philip Murray, President were high UAW and GM officials, including Walter P. Reuther and R. J. Thomas, vice president and president of the union, and C. E. Wilson, vice president of the corporation.

From the meeting came the statement by CIO Headquarters that "arrangements have been made to continue collective bargaining negotiations in Detroit."

Corporation spokesmen on reaffirmed here from Pittsburgh that they would continue negotiations with the union, but they would refuse to give federal conciliators a

(Continued on Page Twelve)

Committees Appointed By Grossman

Named At Regular Monthly Meeting Of Scout Council

At the regular monthly meeting of the Boy Scout Council last night in the Mount Carmel High School, the following appointments were made by District Chairman Harold Grossman: Organization and Extension, John C. Hartsell and Albert Murth; Leadership, Russell Leppert, and Sam Bennett; Camping and Activities, John Potac; Advancement, Sydney Grossman and Frank Bartos; Finance, George Wardrop and Paul Sullivan; Reading Committee, Joseph J. Waligorski; Scout Commissioner, Carl Botka.

On December 19 there will be a commissioners training meeting at which the following will receive training to become commissioners: Elmer Albertini, John Brott, Edward Kretshaut, Alex Bartos.

New troops will be formed in the Flint Methodist Church and the Church of Our Lady, this city and an old troop reorganized at St. Casimir's, Kulpmont.

Cost Of Living Up 33 P. C. Since 1941

WASHINGTON, Dec. 6 (UP)—Stabilization Director John C. Collet today announced regulations for approving wage increases under executive orders issued by the President since the end of the war.

Officials said they did not provide for any blanket price increase because of the relatively small number of workers involved.

Collet advised the War Labor Board that it should consider wage boosts on the basis that the cost of living rose 33 per cent between January, 1941, and September, 1945.

Fort Lauderdale, Florida, on a routine training mission in the skies above the Atlantic. Their route was designed to take them 150 miles (241 km) east, then 40 miles (64 km) north before returning to base. All told, the exercise was supposed to take about two hours.

The squad was led by Lieutenant Charles Taylor, an experienced airman with approximately 2,500 hours logged in the air and who had recently completed a tour of duty in the Pacific theater of World War II aboard the US Navy aircraft carrier USS *Hancock*. Taylor was also an experienced instructor, having moved from the Naval Air Station in Miami where he gave certification training courses similar to the one at NAS Fort Lauderdale. Meanwhile, each of Taylor's thirteen students had logged about 300 hours each; though far from experienced, it is safe to say the men were not unfamiliar with being in the air.

The squad was cleared for takeoff after a preflight inspection revealed that the aircraft were all in order. The only thing missing from each plane was a twenty-four-hour flight clock. This was intentional, as the purpose of the mission was to instruct the airmen in "dead-reckoning," in which a pilot uses his speed, elapsed time, and bearing to calculate his position—handy in the case of a systems malfunction. As such, it was assumed that each man wore his own wristwatch. The weather report from Fort Lauderdale seemed to promise a pleasant flight, describing conditions as "favorable." At 2:00 p.m., the squadron took off, bound for the Atlantic.

An hour into the flight, things started to deteriorate. It seems that at some point during the squadron's turn to the north, Taylor got turned around. According to testimony from another flight instructor leading training in the area, Taylor's squadron was in distress. This instructor made contact with Taylor, who said, "Both my compasses are out, and I am trying to find Fort Lauderdale,

Florida. I am over land but it's broken. I am sure I'm in the Keys, but I don't know how far down, and I don't know how to get to Fort Lauderdale." The squadron's route had them traveling north, but the Florida Keys are due south of Fort Lauderdale. If Taylor's judgment was accurate, they were hundreds of miles off course and traveling in the wrong direction.

The story of Flight 19, which, having been told countless times over the years and has since veered perhaps into legend, goes like this: An hour and fifteen minutes into the flight, the tower at the airbase received a call from Lieutenant Taylor—but not to request landing instructions. Taylor reported, "Cannot see land … We seem to be off course."

The tower, confused that the flight could be lost given the favorable weather, requested the flight's position. Taylor responded, "We cannot be sure where we are. Repeat: Cannot see land."

The tower then lost contact with the group. Ten minutes later, the connection resumed. The leader called in, saying, "We can't find west. Everything is wrong. We can't be sure of any direction. Everything looks strange, even the ocean."

Once again, there was silence—this time lasting for twenty minutes. Once the tower reestablished contact, Taylor was no longer speaking. For reasons unknown, Taylor relinquished his command of the squadron to one of his subordinates. This man radioed in: "We can't tell where we are … everything is … can't make out anything. We think we may be about 225 miles northeast of base." The new leader began gibbering incoherently before saying, "It looks like we are entering white water. We are completely lost." Flight 19 never made contact again.

Although it is questionable how much of the legend of Flight 19 overlaps with the true story, the fact remains that the five aircraft and fourteen men who made up Lieutenant Taylor's squadron were downed in the waters of the Bermuda Triangle on what should have been a routine training exercise led by a capable instructor. What seems likely is that Taylor got turned around at some point during the exercise due to his compass malfunctioning. In order to get his bearing, he mistakenly took an island chain—most likely the cays in the Bahamas, west of Florida—for the Florida Keys. The tower likely took Taylor, an experienced navigator, at his word, and told him to put the setting sun to his port wing and head north past Miami to Fort Lauderdale; but if Taylor was actually in the Atlantic, doing so would have taken him and his men further out into the Atlantic Ocean where they would have run out of fuel and crashed.

Although it seems likely that human error played a significant role in the disappearance of Flight 19, there is still a great deal in the official US Navy report that remains unexplained. Like Columbus, Lieutenant Taylor reported problems with his navigational instruments. His two compasses, which were duplicated in the interest of redundancy in the event that one malfunctioned and which were both inspected prior to takeoff, were both inexplicably inoperable. And, like the *Cyclops* before it, the exact location of the crash remains unknown. No part of Flight 19—no scrap of metal or debris, no human remains—have been recovered from any of the planes despite each being equipped with inflatable life rafts and other survival equipment that had been inspected before the flight.

Between the *Cyclops* and Flight 19, something unusual seems to be happening in the area between Bermuda, Florida, and Puerto Rico. Dozens of other similar tragedies have happened there, both at sea as well as in the air, each of which defies easy explanation. In many cases, the vessels and their crews seem to disappear without a trace, swallowed up by the sea, as though the black waters of the Devil's Triangle will protect its secrets.

The Bimini Road, a network of submerged limestone blocks off the coast of the Bahamas, is thought by some to indicate the location of the mythical lost city of Atlantis.

Exploring the Bermuda Triangle

Disappearances like the USS *Cyclops* and Flight 19 have helped to fuel the mystery surrounding the Bermuda Triangle. The scale of these tragedies, combined with the fact that the wrecks are rarely—if ever—recovered, has sparked decades of speculation about what is going on in the Devil's Triangle. Such explanations range from the practical to the fanciful and fantastic. Everything from UFOs to interdimensional wormholes has been blamed for the disappearances in the Bermuda Triangle. One of the more outlandish theories, for example, involves the sunken city of Atlantis. Some believe that the Bimini Road, an underwater network of rectangular limestone blocks off the coast of the Bahamas, located due southeast of Miami, indicates the location of the lost metropolis. According to legend, the ancient Atlanteans harnessed energy from powerful crystals; when the city became submerged, these crystals went down with it, and today their awesome powers pulsate beneath the waves, causing mechanical and electrical malfunction in modern vessels.

The Bimini Road theory, along with others, make for some pretty interesting sea stories, but there is no evidence that paranormal technology—Atlantean, interdimensional, extraterrestrial, or otherwise—is at work in the Bermuda

Triangle. Instead, there is a multitude of perfectly normal explanations, ranging from natural atmospheric and oceanic phenomenon to simple human error, that helps explain these disappearances. According to the US Coast Guard, which every year is flooded with requests for information about the area of the ocean, "It has been our experience that the combined forces of nature and the unpredictability of mankind outdo science-fiction stories many times each year."

The Sargasso Sea

The Atlantic Ocean in the area of the Bermuda Triangle is home to a number of unique but natural oceanic phenomena that may explain why so many ships have wrecked in its waters without a trace. One of these relates to a section of the ocean known as the Sargasso Sea.

The Sargasso Sea is the only sea in the world not defined at least in part by land boundaries. Instead, it is demarcated only by the number of powerful ocean currents that bound it. Its western boundary consists of the Gulf Stream, a powerful, swift-moving current that originates in the equatorial waters of the Gulf of Mexico. Just as warm air rises, the warm waters of the Gulf Stream surge toward the cold waters off Iceland to find equilibrium. Once part of this current has cooled, it turns south toward Africa, where it is again reheated by the equator. This current, known as the Canary Current after the Canary Islands off Africa's western coast, then heads back toward the Gulf of Mexico. The interplay between these warming and cooling currents forms a rotational system in the Atlantic Ocean known as the North Atlantic Gyre.

The Sargasso Sea—and the Bermuda Triangle—sit almost exactly at the point where these ocean currents converge, which happens to be between Florida and Puerto Rico. The effect this

The calm surface of the Sargasso Sea has made many sailors crossing the Bermuda Triangle feel ill at ease.

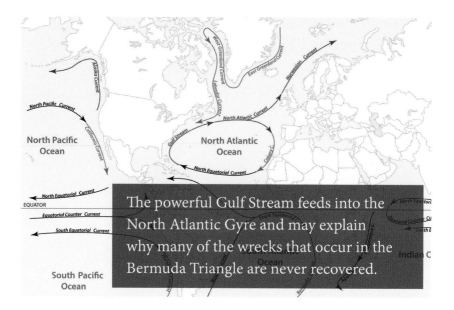

The powerful Gulf Stream feeds into the North Atlantic Gyre and may explain why many of the wrecks that occur in the Bermuda Triangle are never recovered.

convergence has on sea travel is a study in contrasts: on the one hand, the surface of the Sargasso Sea appears tranquil, allowing a unique species of free-floating seaweed called *sargassum* (from which the sea gets its name) to cover the ocean. Many sailors who have traversed the Sargasso Sea have described it as "eerie" and report feeling ill at ease in its placid waters and vast swaths of seaweed patches that seem to cover the surface like grass. In some places, seaweed is so dense and the air so still that a ship can be left completely motionless—stranded in the Sargasso Sea.

Meanwhile, beneath the surface, the enormously powerful Gulf Stream violently courses, accelerating around the tip of Florida and the various Caribbean islands. The Gulf Stream is so powerful that it is possible the current could carry a disabled ship, such as the USS *Cyclops*, or the crew of an airplane that had to land in the water from an emergency, such as Flight 19, out to sea. And if those unfortunate vessels are swallowed by the sea, it's possible the current could carry the debris of ships and aircraft several hundred miles north from their original location before they settle to the bottom. Perhaps the reason no debris from the USS *Cyclops* or Flight 19 has been recovered is because it has all been collected in a vast graveyard in the North Atlantic.

Rogue Waves

The strength of the Gulf Stream may explain why debris from ships and planes that wreck in the Bermuda Triangle are not found, but what causes them to wreck in the first place? One theory points its finger toward a deadly phenomenon: the **rogue wave**. Rogue waves were once considered the stuff of legends and sea shanties. As sailors returned home from long voyages, they described fantastic creatures living beneath the ocean's surface as well as enormous waves that seemed to swallow ships whole like the gaping maw of a monster. It was only recently that scientists have discovered these deadly waves are, in fact, real.

Once the stuff of legends, rogue waves have been documented to reach heights of up to 100 feet (30 m), large enough to sink a boat instantly.

Rogue waves, also known as freak or killer waves, have been described for centuries, and recent scientific documentation proves that these stories are far from legend. Rogue waves are described as sheer walls of water that stretch far higher than surrounding waves. Satellites observing the ocean surface have shown that rogue waves can reach upwards of 100 feet (30 m) from trough to crest. Perhaps more puzzling and frightening is the fact that rogue waves seem to come from out of nowhere; even a small squall with relatively minor wind speeds can produce rogue waves in excess of 50 feet (15 m) that can come from any direction, even directly against the direction of the prevailing waves.

What causes rogue waves remains largely a mystery. There are at least two possible causes: on the one hand, a rogue wave may form when several smaller waves combine over time to form a progressively larger wave; on the other hand, waves from storms going in one direction may combine with the natural direction of a current to form a rogue wave. One thing is clear, however: because rogue waves are the result of a confluence of a number of chaotic variables, including wind speed and the movement of waves, they are highly unpredictable.

The waters between the Gulf of Mexico and the Atlantic Ocean are notoriously violent, spawning approximately a dozen tropical storms and hurricanes each year as well as countless smaller squalls. It is possible that these storms could cause rogue waves large enough to sink a ship or even grab a low-flying aircraft from out of the sky.

Magnetic Malfunction

Sailors and pilots from Christopher Columbus to Lieutenant Charles Taylor have reported malfunction in operation of compasses in the Bermuda Triangle. Accounts of these occurrences have been taken by conspiracy theorists as proof that the Bermuda Triangle is the site of unnatural goings-on. However, this is far from the case. Compasses indicate north by way of a magnet; however, the magnet is attracted to what's known as "magnetic north." There is a significant difference between "true north" and magnetic north. True north corresponds to Earth's North Pole, which is a stationary point in the earth's geography. Magnetic north is the point in Earth's magnetism that moves very slightly over the course of thousands of years.

The degree of difference between the static North Pole and the shifting magnetic north is called "magnetic declination," which varies by as much as 20 degrees depending on one's location. Navigators pinpointing their exact orientation on Earth must account for this variation by "declining" the measurement of their compass with the known degree of declination.

Because Earth is a sphere, there are two points on its surface where magnetic declination equals zero. Here, the imaginary line extending from magnetic north overlaps with that of true north. This is called the agonic line and can cause a compass to seem to behave erratically. One of these spots is the Devil's Sea, off the coast of Japan, and the other is—the Devil's Triangle.

Well, at least it used to be …

The agonic line in the Western Hemisphere currently sits in the Gulf of Mexico, but because the agonic line has been known to be moving westward over the last century, scientists estimate that it likely existed over the Bermuda Triangle during the time of Columbus. This may explain Columbus's confusion noted in his log about unusual compass readings.

THE BERMUDA TRIANGLE IN CONTEXT

There is no question that a large number of ships and planes have wrecked or crashed into the waters of the Devil's Triangle, and more continue to do so every year. This would be unusual if the Bermuda Triangle was the site of the *only* disappearances in the world's oceans, but this is not the case. The fact is that many more go missing all around the world for any number of reasons.

It may seem at first glance that the Bermuda Triangle has an unusually high incidence of disappearance compared to other parts of the ocean; however, it is important to keep in mind that the waters between Miami, Bermuda, and Puerto Rico make up one of the most important and well-used shipping routes in the world. According to historian John Reilly of the US Naval Historical Foundation, "The region is highly traveled and has been a busy crossroads since the early days of European exploration." The Bermuda Triangle may have a large number of tragedies because it is one of the most commonly used routes into and especially out of the Gulf of Mexico, which means that there has been a large amount of traffic sailing through and passing over its waters for centuries. "To say quite a few ships and airplanes have gone down there," Reilly continues, "is like saying there are an awful lot of car accidents on the New Jersey Turnpike—surprise, surprise."

But what about the case of Lieutenant Taylor's compass? By the 1940s, the agonic line was already well west past the Bermuda Triangle, so what caused his malfunction? Generally speaking, navigators are able to account for magnetic declination in their calculations if they know where they are, but the transcript of Flight 19 suggests that Taylor was seriously lost and believed he was somewhere many hundreds of miles away from where he actually was. It is possible that Taylor mistook accurate readings from his two redundant compasses as wrong because he mistakenly believed he was somewhere he was not.

Dropping the A(ir) Bomb

In 2016, newspapers around the United States declared that the mystery of the Bermuda Triangle may have been solved. Scientists analyzing an image that a satellite took over the Bahamas and the coast of Florida on the western edge of the Bermuda Triangle recognized something strange: the photo seemed to depict unusually shaped, hexagonal clouds, with diameters as large as 55 miles (88 km). According to Randall Cerveny, director of the meteorology department at Arizona State University, who also works for the United Nations' World Meteorological Organization, these clouds may be the result of a meteorological phenomenon known as microbursts or, as he called them, "air bombs." Microbursts are extremely strong, downward blasts of air that form as the result of cold air escaping from a thunderstorm. The wind speed of microbursts have been recorded in excess of 100 miles per hour (161 kilometers per hour)—approximately that of a category 2 hurricane. Like rogue waves, microbursts are relatively rare phenomena that can happen at any time and cause extreme damage to anything lying beneath them—such as ships or planes.

Nothing has been proven conclusively about the "honeycomb" clouds over the Bahamas, but that didn't stop news outlets from reporting it as the conclusive scientific explanation for the disappearances. Although it has been widely speculated that these clouds indicate similar high-powered microbursts seen in the North Sea off the coast of Norway, it is not certain whether such phenomena occur in the Bermuda Triangle. The fact is that much remains to be explored and understood.

"Honeycomb" clouds such as these may be the telltale signs of powerful microbursts of wind, also known as "air bombs."

IS THE BERMUDA TRIANGLE A HOAX?

The mystery of the Bermuda Triangle shares a number of similarities with other topics in the paranormal. Because the Bermuda Triangle has no clear explanation, many people believe that there are unexplainable forces at work there, drawing associations to other paranormal subjects such as Bigfoot, UFOs, ghosts, and more. (It has been suggested that the disappearance of Flight 19 was a case of mass alien abduction, a theory which made an appearance in the 1977 science-fiction film *Close Encounters of the Third Kind*.) These theories have caused an equal and opposite skeptical pushback, with many people claiming that the Bermuda Triangle is a **hoax**.

Although the Bermuda Triangle is frequently associated with often-hoaxed paranormal topics, it is not itself a hoax because it has been the site of many true-life, well-documented shipwrecks, plane crashes, and disappearances. In addition, no one who was presumed to have disappeared in the Bermuda Triangle has since come forward to say that they faked their death.

At the same time, it is important to distinguish the lack of proof of a hoax as evidence that paranormal forces are at work in the Bermuda Triangle. Just because the Bermuda Triangle may not be a hoax doesn't necessarily mean that what happens there is caused by anything supernatural. It is simply a place where real tragedies have happened that are unexplained.

The iconic trilithons, or arches, that make up Stonehenge were built nearly five thousand years ago.

The Hanging Stones

T he sea is not the only source of the world's ancient mysteries; land has its own share of secrets. One of the oldest and perhaps the most famous in the whole world is Stonehenge, a prehistoric network of menhirs, or standing stone monuments, located in Wiltshire, England.

Building Stonehenge

The distinctive stone structure known around the world was built in several stages spanning many thousands of years, and archaeological evidence of activity in the area dates back to well before the first stone was raised. Archaeologists have a relatively clear picture of the timeline of Stonehenge's construction by using a process known as **radiocarbon dating** on artifacts found at the site. Radiocarbon dating is a process in which a scientist can determine the age of an organic artifact, such as one of the many trowels made of antler bones that have been found at Stonehenge, by figuring out how much of the object's carbon has decayed. Because carbon decays at a certain rate, scientists can work backwards in order to approximate when an object was first created.

Scientists estimate the age of objects through carbon dating.

The first evidence of activity in the area around Stonehenge takes the form of earthworks. Archaeologists have discovered four or possibly five pits dating back to between 8500 and 7000 BCE. Archaeologists speculate that at least three of these pits may have been used to hold large, totem-like poles made of pine, perhaps similar to those built by Native American tribes in the Pacific Northwest of the United States.

Several thousand years later, around 3500 BCE, two complementary earthworks known as *cursus* monuments were built. These take the form of long, rectangular banks of dirt. The name "cursus" is a Latin word that was used by early British archaeologists, who thought that the rectangular banks were built by the ancient Romans as athletic fields—hence, *cursus*, or "course." (Little did they know that the monuments they were studying dated back to many thousands of years before Rome was even founded.) The largest of the cursus earthworks is known as the Greater or Stonehenge Cursus and stretches 1.7 miles (2.7 km).

Around 3000 BCE, the first known structure of Stonehenge proper was built. This consisted of a circular ditch with both an inner and outer bank of built-up dirt that is 328 feet (100 m) in diameter and surrounds the main site. On the inner side of the ditch are a series of holes that, archaeologists suspect, held standing stones.

The "cursus," once believed to have been built by the ancient Romans, was recently discovered to predate them by several thousand years.

Approximately five hundred years after the circular ditch was built, the main structure of Stonehenge itself began to take shape. At this time, Stonehenge's distinctive standing stones were erected. There are two types of pillar-like stones that make up Stonehenge: the larger sarsens and the smaller bluestones. Over the course of the next five hundred years, the bluestones and sarsens were arranged and rearranged, forming alternately concentric circles and then circles bounded by horseshoe-shaped structures, each of which comprise a series of three-piece arches called **trilithons**.

Few of the arches erected by the ancient builders stand today due to a number of factors over the millennia. Some have been deliberately knocked down and broken up by cultures following Stonehenge's builders, such as the ancient Romans and the medieval Britons, while others have fallen simply as the result of being worn by weather and time. Starting in the twentieth century, there have been a number of restoration projects that have attempted to re-erect the fallen stones.

Today, Stonehenge is cordoned off to the public by a low fence in order to protect against falling stones, though special tours are available outside of public hours that allow visitors to go directly up to the stones.

Guests visiting Stonehenge must keep a safe distance from the arches.

THE NEOLITHIC GRAVEYARD

The name "Stonehenge," like the monument it describes, is itself a puzzle. It is commonly thought to come from the Anglo Saxon words *stan* (stone) and *hengan*, meaning a precipice, such as a cliff, or to hang. Therefore, Stonehenge means "hanging stone." Later writers have taken this etymology to mean that Stonehenge was designed to resemble a gallows—or perhaps was even used *as* a gallows. Perhaps this is why, they have suggested, Stonehenge has also been used as an ancient graveyard.

Indeed, many bodies have been discovered at Stonehenge. Archaeologists have discovered cremated human remains that were interred there as early as 5000 BCE, several thousand years before the first ditch structure was built. The earliest of these remains are found in one of fifty-six so-called Aubrey Pits, which are located just inside the earthwork ditch. Other gravesites are littered around the Stonehenge site, and one body seems to have been decapitated, possibly as a punishment for a capital crime.

Although evidence that Stonehenge was used—at least in part—as a burial ground is significant, archaeologists believe it is highly unlikely that it was a place of execution. For one thing, the decapitated corpse has been identified as an Anglo Saxon, one of ancient Britain's many cultures, and dated back to around 1500 BCE—nearly a millennia since the stones were erected. Because of this, it is unlikely that neither the original builders of Stonehenge nor later civilizations that inhabited the area around it used the site for executions. Furthermore, most of the bodies found in and around Stonehenge were discovered under ceremonial burial mounds and were interred along with certain possessions that would have been prized among these ancient cultures, including especially fine pottery. The care with which these bodies have been buried at Stonehenge indicates that these were likely not thieves, murderers, and other criminals, but respected members of their culture.

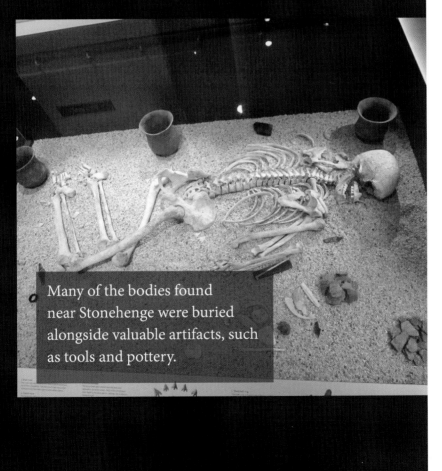

Many of the bodies found near Stonehenge were buried alongside valuable artifacts, such as tools and pottery.

With Stonehenge predating history itself, archaeologists must dig to discover the truth.

CHAPTER FOUR

Secrets in Stone

For as much as we know about the general timeline of Stonehenge's construction, there is still more that we do not know. The ancient Britons who constructed the megalith did not leave an owner's manual, so we are left to guess how and for what purpose it was built. Just as the uncertainty of what goes on under the surface or above the clouds of the Bermuda Triangle, the mystery of Stonehenge has fueled the imagination of countless people throughout the centuries.

Ancient Engineering

Stonehenge has been recognized by the United Nations as a World Heritage Site because it is the largest and most architecturally sophisticated standing stone structure from the prehistoric era. There is no question that Stonehenge, with its massive stone pillars arranged in precise, concentric circles, is an engineering marvel; but considering that it was built thousands of years ago during a time when ancient humans had only rudimentary machines and simple stone tools, isn't Stonehenge so marvelous as to be an impossibility?

The size of the monumental stones at Stonehenge are mind-boggling. The bluestones weigh on average of 4 tons (3.6 metric tons) each—slightly heavier than the average car—while the 30-foot (9 m) sarsens weigh 25 tons (22.6 metric tons)—approximately the same as a school bus, and the heaviest sarsen stones weigh in excess of 50 tons (45.3 metric tons).

Perhaps even more astounding than the sheer mass of the stones is the distances that they were transported before being erected at Stonehenge. Archaeologists have discovered that the larger sarsen stones were quarried in Marlborough Downs near Avebury, in north Wiltshire, approximately 20 and 30 miles (32 to 48 km) north of the site. Meanwhile, archaeologists have pinpointed the source of the bluestones to the Priseli Hills, located in Pembrokeshire, Wales—*140 miles* (225 km) away.

How could the ancient Britons possibly transport, lift, and precisely place these multi-ton stones after transporting them in excess of a hundred miles? To some, the answer is simple: they didn't. There is a theory among certain people that many

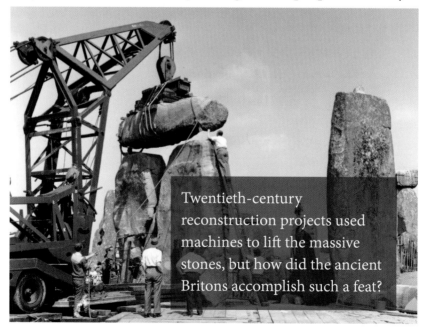

Twentieth-century reconstruction projects used machines to lift the massive stones, but how did the ancient Britons accomplish such a feat?

of the ancient world's greatest architectural achievements were actually accomplished by extraterrestrial visitors—in other words, aliens. This theory, known as the ancient astronaut theory, maintains that ancient humans lacked the tools and knowledge necessary to build the likes of Stonehenge and the Egyptian and Mayan pyramids; instead, they were helped along by well-meaning alien visitors. The ancient astronaut theory has been popularized in particular by the History Channel's *Ancient Aliens* program.

The ancient astronaut theory makes for a good story, but it is universally accepted to be false by the scientific community. The construction of Stonehenge, as incredible of a feat as it is, was well within the capability of ancient peoples. Although the sarsens and bluestones would have been too heavy to transport using timber rollers, archaeologists have concluded that it was possible for a team of ancient people to pull each one along using ropes and a greased wooden sled—albeit slowly. Meanwhile, the stones could have been erected using a crude pulley system, and the crossbeams, known as lintels, put into place by building up an earthen ramp around the standing stones. Although the whole process would have been slow-going and labor-intensive, ancient humans were resourceful and determined.

Stonehenge's Significance

Clearing up how Stonehenge was built raises yet another question: Why would ancient people go through so much trouble to build Stonehenge? There have been a number of theories of Stonehenge's significance (including the outlandish idea that it was built as a landing site for alien spacecraft). Most of the more realistic explanations center around ancient spirituality and religion. Many of the earliest excavations of

Stonehenge, such as the Duke of Buckingham's 1620 dig in the center of the monument, uncovered charred remains of both humans and animals. This discovery points to Stonehenge being used, at least in part, as both a burial site as well as a place for ritual sacrifice.

Many have also observed that the position of Stonehenge corresponds with the two yearly **equinoxes**, which generally mark the beginning of spring and fall. On these days, the rising sun aligns with archways, which may have signified to people gathered at Stonehenge when to sow and reap their harvests. This theory holds that Stonehenge served as a sort of celestial computer or calendar that helped ancient people track the movement of the sun and the passage of the seasons. Given the degree to which ancient people were tied to agriculture, this moment may have held spiritual significance for them.

Although it seems possible or even likely that Stonehenge held some sort of religious significance, it is still unclear exactly what the primary purpose of the megalith was. According to R.J.C. Atkinson, archaeologist from University College, Cardiff, Wales, "Most of what has been written about Stonehenge is nonsense or speculation. No one will ever have a clue what its significance was."

The arrangement of Stonehenge's arches corresponds with the equinox.

WIZARD WORKS

The questions of who built Stonehenge and how has puzzled people for millennia. One of the oldest theories about its construction was proposed in the early twelfth century by the British historian Geoffrey of Monmouth. In 1136, Geoffrey wrote in the *Historia Regum Britanniae* (*History of the Kings of Britain*) that the mythical wizard Merlin, the famous advisor to King Arthur, was responsible for Stonehenge.

According to the *History*, Merlin proposed to the king of England that a monument be erected to mark the graves of the slain princes and kings who had died during the war between the Britons and the Saxons. Merlin recommended that a structure situated in Ireland known as the Giant's Dance, also called the Giant's Ring, be relocated to the south of England. The Giant's Dance, Geoffrey wrote, was originally built by giants who carried stones from Africa. The king agreed and commissioned Merlin and thousands of men to do so. (The Irish, for their part, refused to relinquish their cultural heritage and mounted an army to defend the Dance, but the British defeated them.) When it came time to dismantle the stones, the men found that they could not budge a single one through their combined strength. Merlin laughed and turned his magical abilities on the ring, dismantling it himself stone by stone. When it was rebuilt in England, it was renamed Stonehenge.

In addition to being the oldest, Geoffrey of Monmouth's Merlin theory is also one of the longest held. Many medieval writers and historians believed Geoffrey of Monmouth's version to be true, and it was widely accepted until about the sixteenth century.

MANHATTANHENGE

Stonehenge is not the only monument to embrace the sunset at set points during the year. Manhattan, one of the five boroughs that make up New York City, also features the ability to chart the passage of time. In the early 1800s, New York City's common council passed the Commissioners' Plan of 1811, which established the rectangular grid plan that continues to define Manhattan's geography. The plan set forth a system of (generally) regular north-south–running avenues and east-west–running streets. Many praise the ease with which even a non-native can navigate New York's streets, and the Commissioners' Plan is widely considered one of the greatest achievements in urban planning.

Because Manhattan's streets run east-west, that means that there are two points in the year where the sun shines directly down their broad pavements. Instead of stone menhirs as at Stonehenge, however, the sun that shines in Manhattan is bordered by huge concrete, steel, and glass buildings, giving rise to the term "Manhattanhenge."

Manhattanhenge's "solstices" happen to be Memorial Day (end of May) and baseball's All-Star break (mid-July). Just as the solstices are presumed to have had significance to the early Britons, perhaps the scholars that come after us to study the lost city of Manhattan will presume that these dates held special meaning for the people of New York. According to Neil deGrasse Tyson, "Future anthropologists might conclude that, via the Sun, the people who called themselves Americans worshiped War and Baseball."

"Manhattanhenge" is a unique sight to behold.

There is much that remains unexplained about Stonehenge, so archaeologists will continue to dig for answers.

CHAPTER FIVE

Mysteries Persist

Science has yet to explain everything. In a world where everything seems to be mapped, documented, and recorded, there continue to be enduring mysteries all around us.

Although the Bermuda Triangle may not be unique among the world's oceans, the number of tragedies that have happened there are still significant, and each one seems to defy easy explanation. Perhaps what is most frightening about this expanse of sea named the Devil's Triangle is not that there is any one creature, entity, or phenomenon that happens here, but several. Between towering rogue waves, deadly gusts from "air bombs," confounding mechanical malfunctions, and human error, there are any number of factors that may spell disaster on the open ocean. Because its waters hold their secrets in their dark depths, we may never know for sure. The mysteries of the Bermuda Triangle, along with the rest of the oceans that cover 75 percent of our world, will continue to draw us in, and we must be careful not to be swallowed up in them.

Not all of the world's unexplained places are natural. Some, such as Stonehenge, were made by people. They are monuments to cultures that, though lost to time, have nevertheless left their mark on the world. How exactly our ancient ancestors built and used these structures continues to go unexplained. Instead, we are left with evidence that people—just like any of us—accomplished seemingly impossible feats. Stonehenge, like the pyramids, is part of humanity's legacy. It is not only a monument of a people who have gone before us but also a testament to what people can achieve.

There may not be any inter-dimensional portal in the Bermuda Triangle or some supernatural power at Stonehenge. There may not be anything special about the explained places of the world—except those things that make the world itself special.

Stonehenge will continue to astound and intrigue us.

GLOSSARY

anthropology The field of science that deals with the origins and development of humanity.

capsize To overturn, especially a boat.

cremate A funeral rite in which a dead body is burned and reduced to ashes.

equinox One of two days on which the path of the sun passes Earth's equator, signifying the beginning of spring (vernal) and fall (autumnal).

hoax An intentional attempt to deceive someone.

log A record of events throughout a journey.

megalith An ancient stone monument.

menhir A monumental stone standing either alone or with others.

oceanographer A person who studies the ocean.

phenomenon Something that is observed to exist or happen but whose cause is unknown or uncertain.

radiocarbon dating The process of determining the age of an organic object (something with carbon) by measuring the amount of carbon that has decayed.

rogue wave A spontaneously appearing wave of enormous height and power.

skeptic A person who doubts the claims of another.

squall A sudden, violent windstorm, usually associated with storms on the sea.

trilithon A structure consisting of two vertical standing stones with a horizontal stone placed overtop of them; common among megalithic architecture.

FURTHER INFORMATION

Books

Konstam, Angus. *Ghost Ships: Tales of Abandoned, Doomed, and Haunted Vessels.* London, UK: Lyons Press, 2005.

Pearson, Mike Parker. *Stonehenge: A New Understanding: Solving the Mysteries of the Greatest Stone Age Monument.* New York: The Experiment, 2013.

Pearson, Mike Parker, Joshua Pollard, Colin Richards, Julian Thomas, and Kate Welham. *Stonehenge: Making Sense of a Prehistoric Mystery.* London, UK: Council for British Archaeology, 2016.

Quasar, Gian J. *Into the Bermuda Triangle: Pursuing the Truth Behind the World's Greatest Mystery.* New York: International Marine/McGraw Hill, 2004.

Websites

English Heritage: Stonehenge
http://www.english-heritage.org.uk/visit/places/stonehenge/history
This site features a historical overview of Stonehenge from construction to modern-day, high-resolution photographs, a map of the site, and more.

The History Channel: The Bermuda Triangle
http://www.history.com/topics/bermuda-triangle
The History Channel offers this excellent primer to the history, science, and mysteries of the Bermuda Triangle.

Naval Air Station Fort Lauderdale Museum: The Disappearance of Flight 19 Visual Exhibit
http://www.nasflmuseum.com/flight-19-exhibit.html
The Naval Air Station Museum in Fort Lauderdale, Florida, maintains this website showcasing primary source material associated with the disappearance of Flight 19.

Videos

Nova: Secrets of Stonehenge
http://www.pbs.org/wgbh/nova/ancient/secrets-stonehenge.html
This episode focuses on the mysteries surrounding Stonehenge.

World of Mysteries: The Bermuda Triangle
https://www.youtube.com/watch?v=WLMq5nkmyRM
Watch this video that discusses happenings around the Bermuda Triangle.

BIBLIOGRAPHY

Ashliman, D. L. "Stone Monument Legends." University of
    Pittsburgh, January 25, 2010. http://www.pitt.edu/~dash/
    monuments.html#merlin.

Brennan, Capt. Lawrence B. "The Unanswered Loss of the
    USS *Cyclops*." Naval Historical Foundation, June 13, 2013.
    http://www.navyhistory.org/2013/06/unanswered-loss-uss-
    cyclops-march-1918.

Caesar, Ed. "What Lies Beneath Stonehenge?" Smithsonian.
    com, September 2014. http://www.smithsonianmag.com/
    history/what-lies-beneath-Stonehenge-180952437.

Conradt, Stacy. "The Quick 10: 10 Incidents at the Bermuda
    Triangle." Mental Floss.com, June 6, 2008. http://
    mentalfloss.com/article/18797/quick-10-10-incidents-
    bermuda-triangle.

Fritz, Angela. "The 'Bermuda Triangle mystery' isn't solved,
    and this scientist didn't suggest it was." *Washington Post*,
    October 25, 2016. https://www.washingtonpost.com/
    news/capital-weather-gang/wp/2016/10/25/the-bermuda-
    triangle-mystery-isnt-solved-and-this-scientist-didnt-
    suggest-it-was.

"History of Stonehenge." English Heritage.org.uk, http://www.
    english-heritage.org.uk/visit/places/stonehenge/history.

"How Was Stonehenge Built?" *Stonehenge: The Age of the Megaliths*. Bradshaw Foundation.com, http://www.bradshawfoundation.com/stonehenge/construction.php.

"Lynch, Thomas, Jr., (1749–1779)." Biographical Directory of the United States Congress: 1774–Present." Congress.gov, http://bioguide.congress.gov/scripts/biodisplay.pl?index=L000535.

McDonell, Michael. "Flight 19: 'Lost Patrol.'" *Naval Aviation News*. Naval History and Heritage Command, June 1973. https://www.history.navy.mil/browse-by-topic/disasters-and-phenomena/flight-19/flight-19-lost-patrol.html.

"The North Atlantic Gyre." European Space Agency. Accessed October 26, 2016, https://www.esa.int/SPECIALS/Eduspace_Weather_EN/SEM1HYK1YHH_0.html.

Owen, James. "Stonehenge Was Cemetery First and Foremost, Study Says." National Geographic News, May 29, 2008. http://news.nationalgeographic.com/news/2008/05/080529-stonehenge-cemetery.html.

Pearson, Mike Parker. *Stonehenge: A New Understanding: Solving the Mysteries of the Greatest Stone Age Monument*. New York: The Experiment, 2013.

Quasar, Gian J. *Into the Bermuda Triangle: Pursuing the Truth Behind the World's Greatest Mystery.* New York: International Marine/McGraw Hill, 2004.

"Skeleton Challenges Ideas on Stonehenge." ABC News, July 15, 2016. http://abcnews.go.com/Technology/story?id=120110&page=1.

"Stonehenge." Encyclopedia Britannica, https://www.britannica.com/topic/Stonehenge.

"Stonehenge 'bluestone' quarries confirmed 140 miles away in Wales." University College London, December 7, 2015. https://www.ucl.ac.uk/news/news-articles/1215/071215-stonehenge-bluestone-quarries.

Tyson, Neil deGrasse. "Manhattanhenge." American Museum of Natural History, http://www.amnh.org/our-research/hayden-planetarium/resources/manhattanhenge.

Weisberger, Mindy. "No, 'Honeycomb' Clouds Don't Explain Bermuda Triangle Mystery." LiveScience.com, October 24, 2016. http://www.livescience.com/56622-bermuda-triangle-air-bombs-not-likely.html.

"What is the Sargasso Sea?" National Ocean Service, November 3, 2015. http://oceanservice.noaa.gov/facts/sargassosea.html.

"What is a rogue wave?" National Ocean Service, December 8, 2014. http://oceanservice.noaa.gov/facts/roguewaves.html.

INDEX

Page numbers in **boldface** are illustrations. Entries in **boldface** are glossary terms.

ABOUT THE AUTHOR

Andrew Coddington has written a number of books for Cavendish Square Publishing on a variety of topics, including history and the paranormal. In addition to *The Bermuda Triangle, Stonehenge, and Unexplained Places*, he has also written *Aliens, UFOs, and Unexplained Encounters* and *The Hope Diamond, Cursed Objects, and Unexplained Artifacts* in the Paranormal Investigations series. He lives in Buffalo, New York, with his wife and dog.